Text © 2010 by Janet Severi Bristow and
Victoria A. Cole-Galo
Photographs © 2010 by Jeff McNamara
Illustrations © 2010 by The Taunton Press, Inc.

All rights reserved.

This material was previously published in the
book *The Crocheted Prayer Shawl Companion 37
Patterns to Embrace Inspire & Celebrate Life*
(ISBN 978-1-60085-293-0)
First published in this format 2012

The Taunton Press
Inspiration for hands-on living®

The Taunton Press, Inc., 63 South Main Street
PO Box 5506, Newtown, CT 06470-5506
e-mail: tp@taunton.com

Interior Design: Kimberly Adis
Illustrator: Christine Erickson
Photographer: Jeff McNamara

Threads® is a trademark of The Taunton Press,
Inc., registered in the U.S. Patent and
Trademark Office.

The following names/manufacturers appearing
in *Crocheted Prayer Shawls* are trademarks:
Caron®, Red Heart®, Rosario 4®

Printed in the United States of America
10 9 8 7 6 5 4 3 2 1

CONTENTS

Where to Begin   3

Original Crocheted Prayer Shawl   9

Textured Beaded Shawl   11

Granny Square Edged Shawl   15

Portuguese Inspired Shawl   17

Milk Fiber Shawl   21

Genevieve's Journey Shawl   23

Topaz Shawl   27

Cape Cod Shawl   29

Crocheting Abbreviations   30

Standard Yarn Weights   31

WHERE TO BEGIN

TO TANGIBLY WRAP SOMEONE IN YOUR PRAYERS AND BEST wishes for them is a blessing. Too often, words cannot convey our feelings of love and concern for another, but to drape a shawl made by the work of your hands and the prayers of your heart around someone's shoulders speaks volumes. The process of making a prayer shawl is different from the average crochet project because it is a spiritual practice for the shawl maker. One creates a safe haven, a private space into which the wearer can escape for rest, relaxation, and renewal. As such, the focus and intention takes on more significance.

To Whom Will the Shawl Go?

Be it a family member, friend, or colleague, it seems we all know someone who could use a prayer shawl. These days especially, with so much turmoil over job losses, health alerts, and general uneasiness about the future, the world needs comforting. Without hesitation, any of us could pick up our crochet hook and know who will receive our next shawl. Barbara, a member of our message board, wrote: "I learned right from the start that the shawls are owned before they are made." So,

even if things change when we're finished and a more immediate need arises, trust that your shawl goes to the person meant to receive it. Then, start again.

Considering Color

Color talks. The moment we see a color, it speaks to us. A bright red or orange can lift a mood; blues can calm and soothe; dark colors bring a sense of being enfolded; pastels and neutrals offer comfort. In this book, we offer a page on the symbolism of color as a general guideline, but let your intuition and imagination guide you in the selection process. Be willing to work with a color that you've never used. It has been our experience that you may be surprised by the choice and gain a new favorite color by the time you've finished the shawl.

Which Fiber?

The texture of a shawl is important. We want it to be soft, comforting the wearer in its embrace. If you know the receiver of the shawl you're making, take time in the selection process. There are new yarns on the market today made of intriguing fibers such as soy, bamboo, corn, and even milk! Some are made from recycled silk saris or recycled plastic bottles in blends with acrylic and polyester. Their yarn wrappers, too, are made from recycled paper. Even if you don't know who will receive the shawl, it's the perfect opportunity to consider "stepping out of the box" and experiment!

If the pattern you choose is a simple one, select a yarn with a bumpier texture, such as a bouclé. In this type of shawl, the yarn is the star. With a more complex pattern, choose a smoother, worsted weight yarn to show off the design. When creating a special shawl for family and friends, consider the luxury of cashmere, silk, mohair, or alpaca. And what to do with all the remnants? Mix them and create a stunning, one-of-a-kind work of art with bands of different colors and fibers, crocheted either widthwise or lengthwise. Crocheters have the ability to create lovely floral motifs, and this might be the time to create a few flowers with which to embellish the shawl. Once you've experimented with all the different choices, you'll become comfortable with the process of making a prayer shawl. Enjoy the experience, expressing your creativity and relaxing into the art of crochet.

The Setting

While the spiritual component of making a shawl has already begun with the selection of the yarn, it is perhaps most evident in the practice of sitting down to prayerfully crochet the shawl. Creating a small, meaningful ritual will help set the intention for shawl making. Begin by gathering the yarn, tools, a candle and matches, a journal and pen, and a favorite poem, reading, or prayer. Find a quiet, comfortable spot, preferably away from distractions, either inside or outdoors. It's also

nice to have on hand a beverage, mild-scented hand lotion, and music playing softly in the background.

Sit quietly and take a few, deep, cleansing breaths; center yourself and think about what you're about to do and for whom. Light the candle and massage the lotion into your hands, thanking them for all they do for you every day. Record the date in your journal, and as you crochet, jot down any insights, thoughts, and ideas that come to mind. These can be incorporated into a note to the recipient, or they might be the beginnings of a prayer, blessing, or poem.

The journal can also be a source of meditation for you, a way to reflect and pray for the recipients of your lovingly made shawls for years to come. When making a shawl for a friend, some groups keep a journal of each member's thoughts and best wishes, passing it on with the shawl. Lay your hand on the yarn and crochet hook, recite a blessing, poem, or prayer, or just sit quietly. Then start your beginning chain.

Keep the recipient in your thoughts and prayers as you crochet. Imagine a time in your life when you felt safe and comforted, perhaps lovingly enfolded in a blanket by someone who cared for you. Swaddle and enfold the recipient in your prayers as the shawl unfolds from the yarn. Pray that they will feel peace, contentment, and loving energy every time they wrap it around themselves.

Adornments

After the body of the shawl is finished, think about embellishments and adornments. Fringe or tassels are lovely. This can be a prayerful process, as a blessing or wish is offered with each piece of yarn affixed to an edge. Try enlisting the help of a loved one, allowing them to make their own contribution to this special gift. In some groups, there are folks who aren't able to make a shawl, but are more than happy to work on its fringe.

Medals, charms, and beads add to the beauty of a shawl and can become a source of meditation. There are many charms from which to choose, such as religious symbols, hearts, butterflies, angels, or stars. For example, add a flower charm if both you and the recipient enjoy gardening, or a seashell if you share a love of the ocean. For more ideas, see the Symbolism page of www.shawlministry.com.

If the shawl is a group gift, ask each person to contribute her or his own memento. Invite the recipient to add beads and charms of her or his own. Lockets containing photos are especially meaningful. The more precious trinkets can be attached to a jewelry clasp so they can be removed if the shawl needs to be cleaned. Catholics might appreciate the addition of 10 beads on each side of the shawl on which to say a decade or two of the rosary.

A Blessing

Before the shawl is sent on its way, offer up a final blessing. You may choose to write your own blessing or use a favorite prayer or poem. This could be a group process, or perhaps one of your members would like to volunteer to compose one. For more ideas, visit the Prayers page of www.shawlministry.com. If you belong to a group, place the finished shawls on a table, gather around, lay your hands on them, and say a blessing in unison. Think about what you'd like to say to the recipients of your shawls. Reread your journal. Compose a note or a letter that explains the meaning behind the prayer shawl, as well as the reason it's being given and by whom. Some groups or individuals go into detail, explaining the meaning of the color and combination of stitches; others include a simple tag printed with a blessing tied to the shawl. There are special-order cloth labels or printed ribbon, found on the Internet or through a craft or fabric store. These can be sewn onto the shawl as a way of identifying the giver or group. Even a simple, heartfelt, handwritten note can be included—the choice is yours. Some groups bless their shawls during a church service. Doing so includes the members of the congregation who don't make the shawls. This way, your whole faith community becomes involved.

Presentation

Circumstances dictate the actual presentation of a prayer shawl. If you are delivering the shawl in person, simply give the shawl to the recipient, explaining what it is and why you want her or him to have it. If you feel comfortable, consider saying a blessing, prayer, or poem as you drape the shawl around the receiver's shoulders. Don't worry if the person doesn't seem as receptive at first; sometimes it takes a while for it all to sink in. This could be an opportunity for quiet conversation, reflection, even shared tears. Most important, it is a sacred moment in which the giver, the receiver, and all present are blessed.

If a group of friends is presenting a shawl, gather around the recipient with everyone placing a hand on the shawl as you read the blessing in unison. Our first shawl was for a friend going through a divorce. Although the recipient wasn't present for the blessing, a group of sister friends gathered together, each taking turns wrapping up in the shawl and sharing a blessing, either spoken aloud or said silently in our hearts. Later, as it was wrapped around our friend's shoulders, she was told of the prayers and good wishes that had been prayed into it by those who cared for her.

Always let the circumstances, the place, and the personality of the receiver guide you. What we've described above is a wonderful opportunity for sharing and blessing for all involved. Make sure there is enough time for this wonderful ritual. That being said, there will be occasions when you won't be involved in a formal presentation. Sometimes shawls are picked up by others, or they're mailed to

the recipient. However a shawl is given, trust that it will be a sacred moment, and one that happens at just the right time.

Packaging

There are many ways to package the shawls. Here are some attractive as well as practical options:

• Place in a decorative gift bag. Although less durable, these also hold any items you'd like to include and are attractive for presentations done in person. Some groups buy solid-colored bags, which are then decorated by the youth of their faith community.

• Make a pouch from remnant fabric or yarn. This type of bag creates a little pillow when holding the shawl and offers comfort.

• Place in a 2-gallon zip-top plastic bag. These types of bags make the shawls easy to store, protect a ministry's collection of shawls until they are given away, and hold tags, letters, cards, and sachets. They're also handy for deliveries to hospitals and nursing homes.

• We've seen new cake boxes used, donated to a church group by a local bakery. The boxes have a clear window that shows the color of the shawl.

• Simply wrap the shawl in pretty tissue paper, wrapping paper, or fabric, tied with a piece of yarn.

It's Blessed to Receive as Well

There might be a time when you, as a shawl maker, may receive a shawl, too. This can be a surprising and humbling experience to those of us used to being on the giving end. If an occasion arises in which someone gives you a prayer shawl, allow yourself to be a willing recipient. Allow someone else to minister to you. Pray for the maker of your shawl whenever you wrap that gift of love around you. Feel all the loving energy and prayer that went into its making, and receive the blessing. What a wonderful, full-circle moment to experience being both the giver and receiver.

Gentle Shawl Making

Those of us with health issues that impede our crocheting—carpal tunnel syndrome, fibromyalgia, arthritis, and others—can still be active participants in the Prayer Shawl Ministry. Devices such as portable looms can make shawl making easy on the hands. Folks are thrilled when they find they can make shawls with these aids. Start simply, slowly, and prayerfully. Do what you can in small blocks of time, putting the work aside when you need to rest. You may want to do just part of a shawl and pass it on to someone else. Or, you could prayerfully concentrate on the fringe or border of a shawl that someone else has made. If you belong to a group, volunteer to write notes, keep track of the shawls, or put together a group scrapbook. The most important component of this ministry is prayer, which doesn't require physical strength, just a desire of the heart.

RITA GLOD DEVELOPED THIS CROCHETED SHAWL pattern to follow its knitted sister pattern and brought it to her local Prayer Shawl Ministry in Connecticut. Like the knit and purl stitches, single crochets and double crochets combine in the symbolism of threes.

FROM
Rita Glod
Stafford Springs, Connecticut

ORIGINAL
CROCHETED PRAYER SHAWL

Skill Level
Easy

Finished Measurements
18 in. x 70 in., excluding fringe

Yarn
- Light Weight Yarn (CYCA 3), approx. 1,000 yd. Black
- Shawl shown in yarn from Independence Farm of Thomaston, Connecticut (100% alpaca; 250 yd./4 oz.), 4 skeins Bay Black

Hook
- Size J/10/6 mm (or size needed to obtain gauge)

Optional Materials
Stone chip beads and clear nylon or elastic beading filament to embellish tassels as shown on page 10 in photo

Gauge
- 11 sts and 5 dc rows = 4 in. in patt st

Note: Ch-3 counts as 1 dc throughout.

DIRECTIONS
Ch 63 (or desired width) loosely.

Row 1: Sc in 2nd ch from hook and in each ch across. Ch 3, turn. (62 sc)

Row 2: Sk 1st sc, dc in each sc across. Ch 3, turn. (62 dc counting t-ch)

Row 3: Sk 1st dc, dc in each dc across. Ch 3, turn.

Row 4: Rep Row 3. Ch 1, turn.

Row 5: Sc in each dc across. Ch 3, turn.

Rep Rows 2–5 for pattern until work measures 70 in. or desired length, ending with a Row 5. End off.

TASSEL FRINGE
Cut 144 22-in. lengths of yarn. Fold each strand in half, then attach 8 strands of fringe in a group, 9 groups evenly spaced along each short side. Tie in an overhand knot close to the shawl, adding a strand of beads if desired.

A Yarn Reflection

Having never crocheted with alpaca fiber before, I was delighted to use freshly spun yarn from a beautiful six-year-old huacaya alpaca named Inca Bay, owned by a colleague of mine. The yarn came in twisted skeins, which I wound into the most luxuriously soft balls with which to work. This animal has the sweetest face, and I couldn't help thinking about the last time I saw alpacas at a farm in New Hampshire during a fiber festival.

A llama was the shepherdess, and the alpacas flocked around her as she led them back into the barn. It was remarkable how the alpacas trusted the llama, a trait I found endearing.

To enhance this natural fiber, I chose to embellish the shawl with beautiful green Jasper chips said to be worn for protection. Right now, Inca Bay is ready to deliver a baby, so I wove some extra prayers into the shawl that the delivery will go smoothly, producing a healthy and equally beautiful offspring.

—JANET BRISTOW
Farmington, Connecticut

SAY A LITTLE PRAYER

*As I start this shawl, I say a little prayer
In hopes this shawl will be worn,
And not thrown neatly on a chair.
I say a little prayer that the Lord grants
your intentions that only you know.
I hope this shawl gives you comfort wherever you go.
So, when you are happy, or sad, or think no one cares,
Wrap this shawl around you and say a little prayer.
Hope, faith, and love is in
each stitch I make from beginning to end.
And with all the prayers I pray
with this shawl that I send.
I pray that you know that the Lord is always there.
As I am finished with this shawl, I say a little prayer.*

—TISH HOAR
MOUNT VERNON, OHIO

I DEVELOPED THIS PRAYER SHAWL FOR A CHURCH friend who is blind. The texture of the stitches and the use of beads and charms on the ends allowed her to experience the prayer shawl in a special way. The shawl features a repeat pattern of three rows of double crochet and one row of popcorn stitches and double crochet, with the popcorn stitch occurring in every third stitch. An assortment of beads and charms on the two ends also provides texture and interest to the shawl.

FROM
Jan Bass
Hayward, California

TEXTURED BEADED SHAWL

Skill Level
Easy

Finished Measurements
22 in. x 45 in.

Yarn
- Bulky Weight Yarn (CYCA 5), approx. 900 yd. Yellow
- Shawl shown on page 12 in SWTC Inc. Saphira (100% superwash merino wool; 132 yd./3.5 oz.), 7 skeins #579

Hook
- Size K/10.5/6.5 mm (or size needed to obtain gauge)

Optional Materials
- Coordinating beads or charms with large enough opening for yarn to pass through.

Gauge
- 10 sts and 6 rows = 4 in. in patt st

Special Stitches
- **Pc** = popcorn st: Work 4 dc in specified dc, remove hook from loop, insert hook into the 1st of 4 dcs. Reinsert hook into the loop of the 4th dc and draw through the loop of the first dc. Ch 1. One pc made.

Note on use of beads and charms:
- If the shawl is to be given to a person who is visually impaired, consider using beads and charms of various shapes and sizes for tactile interest. Bead colors can be coordinated with the yarn color, so the finished shawl will look nice for those who are sighted.

continued

TEXTURED BEADED SHAWL

- Use beads and charms that have a large enough hole for the yarn and a small hook to pass through them.

- The beads and charms for the starting sc row can be slipped onto the yarn prior to starting the shawl and moved along the yarn until ready to incorporate into the starting sc row. The beads and charms for the final sc row can either be slipped on from the end of the yarn, making sure there is enough yarn to crochet the sc row, or a new length of yarn can be added just before the finishing sc row with the beads and charms slipped onto this length of yarn. Push beads and charms to the RS of the shawl.

- The beads and charms can either be worked into the sc themselves or be placed between sc stitches. Place a bead or charm every third stitch, starting with either the third sc, which will align with the popcorn stitches, or starting with the second sc, which will be offset slightly from the popcorn stitches. The latter will use one more bead/charm than the former on each end. (20 or 21 beads/charms per end; 40 or 42 beads/charms total)

DIRECTIONS

Ch 63 loosely (multiple of 3 + 2 + 1 for foundation ch).

Row 1: Incorporating beads if desired (see note), sc in 2nd ch from hook and in each ch across. Ch 3, turn. (62 sc)

Rows 2–3: Sk 1st st, dc in next st and each st across. Ch 3, turn. (62 dc)

Row 4 (RS): Rep Row 2, working in back loops only.

Row 5: Rep Row 2, working in front loops only.

Row 6: Working in both loops sk 1st dc, dc in next dc, * pc in next dc, dc in each of next 2 dc. Rep from * across. Ch 3, turn. (42 dc and 20 pc)

Row 7: Sk 1st dc, dc in next dc, * dc in ch-1 of pc, dc in each of next 2 dc. Rep from * across. Ch 3, turn. (62 dc)

Rep Rows 4–7 for pattern until work measures 44 in. or 1 in. less than desired length, ending with a Row 5.

Next Row: Sk 1st dc, dc in next dc and in each dc across. Ch 1, turn.

Final Row: Incorporating beads if desired, sc in each dc across. End off.

T HIS SHAWL INCORPORATES A VARIATION ON the granny square along the edges. It's a great way to experiment with a motif other than the classic granny square. The shawl is shown in worsted weight yarn. Sport weight can be used for a lighter shawl.

FROM
Janet Bristow
Farmington, Connecticut

GRANNY SQUARE–EDGED SHAWL

Skill Level
Easy

Finished Measurements
24 in. x 70 in.

Yarn
• Medium Weight Yarn (CYCA 4), approx. 1,455 yd. in three colors (945 yd. color A, 630 yd. color B, and 315 yd. color C)
• Shawl shown in Caron® Simply Soft (100% acrylic; 315 yd./6 oz.), 3 skeins #9738 Violet (color A), and Lion Brand Vanna's Choice (100% acrylic; 170 yd./3.5 oz.), 2 skeins #134 Terra Cotta (color B), and 1 skein #170 Pea Green (color C)

Hooks
• Size D/3/3.25 mm and F/5/3.75 mm (or sizes needed to obtain gauge)

Optional Materials
• 16 beads or decorative shank buttons

Gauge
• 11 sts and 6 rows = 4 in. in patt st for Body

Notes:
• **Ch-3 counts as 1 dc throughout.**
• **In Motif, ch-5 counts as 1 dc + 2 ch.**

DIRECTIONS

MOTIF
Make 8: in this color order, 4 reversing colors A and B

With size D hook and color A, ch 4, sl st in 1st ch to form ring.

Rnd 1: Ch 3, 15 dc in ring, join with sl st in top of beg ch. (16 dc, ch-3 counts as 1 dc here and throughout)

Rnd 2: Sl st between beg ch-3 and next dc of prev rnd, ch 5 (counts as 1 dc + ch 2), [dc in between next 2 dc, ch 2] 15 times, join rnd with sl st in 3rd ch of beg ch-5. (16 ch-2 sp)

continued

GRANNY SQUARE— EDGED SHAWL

Rnd 3: Sl st in next ch-2 sp, ch 3, 2 dc in same sp, [ch 1, sk next dc, 3 dc in next ch-2 sp] 15 times, ch 1, sk next dc, join rnd with sl st in top of beg ch. End off. (16 3-dc shells)

Rnd 4: Join color B in any ch-1 sp, sc in same sp, *[ch 3, sk next 3 dc, sc in next ch-1 sp] 3 times, ch 5 (corner loop made), sc in next ch-1 sp. Rep from * 3 times more, omitting final sc of last rep, join rnd with sl st in first sc. (12 ch-3 loops + 4 ch-5 corner loops)

Rnd 5: Sl st in next ch-3 sp, ch 3, 2 dc in same sp, [ch 1, sk next sc, 3 dc in next ch-3 sp] twice, ch 1, [5 dc, ch 2, 5 dc] in next ch-5 sp, *[ch 1, sk next sc, 3 dc in next ch-3 sp] 3 times, ch 1, [5 dc, ch 2, 5 dc] in next ch-5 sp. Rep from * 2 times more, ch 1, sk next sc, join rnd with sl st in top of beg ch (76 dc/19 per side). End off.

Rnd 6: Join color C in any ch-2 corner sp, ch 3, [tr, dc] in same sp, *[dc between next 2 dc] 4 times; ** dc in next ch-1 sp, [dc in between next 2 dc] twice **; rep from ** to ** twice more; dc in next ch-1 sp, [dc in sp between next 2 dc] 4 times, [dc, tr, dc] in next corner ch-2 sp. Rep from * 3 times more, omitting final [dc, tr, dc] of last rep, join rnd with sl st in top of beg ch. (80 dc/20 per side + 4 tr) End off.

JOINING

Make 2 strips of 4 squares each, alternating color pattern.

With RS together, whip st squares together through front loops only using color C.

BODY

Hold 1 assembled strip with RS facing and long edge on top, join color C in first tr.

Row 1 (RS): Ch 3, * dc in next 20 dc, dc in next seam, rep from * 3 times more; dc in last tr (85 dc). End off.

Row 2 (RS): With RS facing, join color A in top of beg ch-3 of prev row, ch 4, tr in each dc to end. Ch 3, turn. (85 tr)

Row 3 (WS): Sk 1st tr, dc in each tr to end. Ch 4, turn.

Row 4: Sk 1st dc, tr in each dc to end. Ch 3, turn.

Rep Rows 3 & 4 for patt until shawl is 64 in. or 6 in. less than desired length, ending with a Row 3. End off.

Last Row: With RS facing and color C, rep Row 1.

ATTACH SECOND STRIP

With RSs facing each other, whip st 2nd strip to just-finished shawl body through front loops only using color C lining up sts as you go.

OPTIONAL EDGING

Hold shawl with RS facing and long side at top. With size F hook and color of choice, join yarn in first dc. *Sk next 2 dc, 5 dc in next dc, sk next 2 dc, sl st in next dc. Rep from * around shawl (counting end st of each row of center section as a dc), adjust sts slightly so that last sl st is made in joining sl st. End off.

FINISHING

Weave in all ends. Block if desired.

Affix beads or decorative buttons to the center hole of each motif. If using buttons, stitch 2 back to back so they can be viewed from either side.

THE INSPIRATION FOR THIS SHAWL COMES FROM

FROM
Vicky Galo
Berlin, Connecticut

the look of the yarn and its country of origin. It comes from the Rosarios 4® Factory in Mira de Aire, Portugal, my husband's birthplace. The town of Mira de Aire is nestled at the base of a large mountain. Growing on the side of the mountain are wild olive trees. The green in the yarn reminds me of the olive tree leaves, and the orange hue reminds me of the stalactite and stalagmite stones that can be found deep within the caves or *grutas* of the mountain. As the "double crochet, chain 1" pattern began to reveal itself, I noticed that the double crochet stitch appears to slightly twist, much like the trunk of an olive tree with its arms reaching up to support the row above.

PORTUGUESE INSPIRED SHAWL

Skill Level
Easy

Finished Measurements
18 in. x 78 in., excluding fringe

Yarn
- Medium Weight Yarn (CYCA 4), approx. 1,080 yd. Rust/Green
- Shawl shown on page 18 in Rosarios 4® Sole Latte (100% milk fiber; 180 yd./3.5 oz.), 6 skeins #05 Autumn/Winter

Hook
- Size H/8/5.0 mm (or size needed to obtain gauge)

Gauge
- 16 sts and 8 rows = 4 in. in patt st

Note: Ch-4 counts as 1 dc + ch-1 throughout.

DIRECTIONS
Ch 88 loosely (any odd number of sts + 1 for foundation ch).

Row 1: Sc in 2nd ch from hook and in each ch across. Ch 4, turn. (87 sc)

Row 2: Sk 2 sc, dc in next sc, *ch 1, sk 1 sc, dc in next sc. Rep from * across. Ch 1, turn. (44 dc counting t-ch)

continued

PORTUGUESE INSPIRED SHAWL

Row 3: Sc in 1st dc, *ch 1, sk ch-1 sp, sc in next dc. Rep from * across, placing last dc in 3rd ch of t-ch. Ch 4, turn. (44 sc)

Row 4: Sk ch-1 sp, dc in next sc, * ch 1, sk ch-1 sp, dc in next sc. Rep from * across. Ch 1, turn. (44 dc counting t-ch)

Rep Rows 3 and 4 for pattern, until work measures 77 ½ in. or ½ in. less than desired length, ending with a Row 4.

Last Row: Sc in each dc and ch-1 sp across. End off. (87 sc)

Weave in ends.

FRINGE

Cut 174 12-in. strands of yarn. Fold each strand in half, then attach fringe in each st on both short sides. Tie groups of 3 in an overhand knot close to the shawl.

Warming Shawl

A few years ago, I became involved with the Kairos Outside Ministry, which is for women whose lives have been impacted by incarceration. I was one of the spiritual directors for the first KO Weekend in Maine. During the team meetings, a woman was working on a shawl, and she explained the Prayer Shawl Ministry. I told my mother (who was 89 years old at the time) about it, and she made several shawls for the weekend guests. She also surprised me with one, which I wore for the first time during that retreat weekend.

I was to lead a ceremony with the theme of love. I was a little nervous, and the room was a bit chilly. I put on my shawl and prayed that I would feel the love that Mom had knit into the shawl for me. As I gave my talk and began to minister to each of the guests, I got warmer, and warmer, and warmer. I had to take off the shawl because I was too hot and was being distracted by the heat of my body. It was then that I realized the heat was actually my experiencing the love and prayers that were knit into the shawl. I was enveloped in love. I had so much love to give away to these women!

My prayer is always that others feel the love that is knit into their shawls, just as I was overwhelmed with the love knit into mine by my mother.

—MARY RICH, Waterboro, Maine

INTO MY PRAYER

*Heart beats, in time with breath as
the hook swirls among yarn
sliding through fingers,
into my
prayer.*

—JANET SEVERI BRISTOW
FARMINGTON, CONNECTICUT

READ THE LABEL OF THIS YARN CAREFULLY. "MILK fiber." We've heard of hay being spun into gold, and bamboo, soy, and corn being transformed into decadent textural fibers, but who would have ever thought of milk? May this shawl be a reminder for you to nurture your soul.

FROM
Vicky Galo
Berlin, Connecticut

MILK FIBER SHAWL

Skill Level
Easy

Finished Measurements
17 in. x 78 in., excluding fringe

Yarn
- Medium Weight Yarn (CYCA 4), approx. 624 yd. Blue
- Shawl shown in Rosarios 4 Cappuccino Cream (70% Australian wool/30% milk fiber; 104 yd./1.75 oz.), 6 skeins #49

Hook
- Size I/9/5.50 mm (or size needed to obtain gauge)

Gauge
- 3 loops and 4 rows = 4 in. in pattern st. Gauge is not critical in this pattern.

Special Stitches
- **Knots** = Rigmarole or Lover's Knot stitch: *Extend loop on hook until it is 1 in. long or desired length, ch 1 while grasping base of st so working yarn can't pull on loop and length is maintained, sc in back/single loop only of extended ch. Rep from * until desired number of knot sts is made.

DIRECTIONS
Row 1: Ch 2, sc in 2nd ch from hook, work 36 knots. Turn.

Row 2: Sc in 5th sc from hook, *work 2 knots, sk 1 sc, sc in next sc. Rep from * to end. Turn. (17 loops)

Row 3: *Work 2 knots, sk 1 sc, sc in next sc. Rep from * to end. Turn. (17 loops)

Rep Row 3 for pattern until shawl measures 78 in. or desired length. End off. Weave in ends.

FRINGE
Cut 68 12-in. lengths of yarn. Fold each strand in half, then attach two strands of fringe in each loop. Tie groups of 2 in an overhand knot close to the shawl, then add another row of knots.

GENEVIEVE'S JOURNEY SHAWL

KATHLEEN TAYLOR DESIGNED THIS BEAUTIFUL LACY crochet shawl. Her shawl is dedicated to her daughter-in-law, Genevieve, who recently relocated to a different state. The shawl is light and airy without being fussy, the perfect wrap for a cool summer evening.

Skill Level
Intermediate

Finished Measurements
20 in. x 82 in. after blocking

Yarn
- Super Fine Yarn Weight (CYCA 1), approx. 1,200 yd. Pale Green
- Shawl shown in Decadent Fibers Savory Socks (90% merino wool/ 10% nylon; 400 yd./3.5 oz.), 3 skeins Sage

Hook
- Size F/5/3.75 mm (or size needed to obtain gauge)

Gauge
- 20 sts and 14 rows = 4 in. in patt st. unblocked

Note: The body of the shawl is worked symmetrically from the center. The borders are worked lengthwise after the body of the shawl is completed.

DIRECTIONS

SHAWL BODY
Ch 72 loosely (multiple of 10 + 1 + 1 for foundation ch).

Row 1: Sc in the 2nd ch from hook, sc in the next ch, *ch 3, sk 3 ch, (dc, ch 2, dc) in next ch, ch 3, sk 3 ch, sc in the next 3 ch. Rep from * across, end with sc in last 2 ch. Turn. (7 dc shells)

Row 2: Ch 1, sc in 1st sc, *ch 4, sk ch-3 sp, 5 dc in ch-2 space, ch 4, sk next sc, sc in the next sc. Rep from * across. Turn.

continued

KATHLEEN TAYLOR'S
GENEVIEVE'S JOURNEY SHAWL

Row 3: Ch 7, sk ch-4 sp, *sc in each of next 5 dc, ch 7, sk 2 ch-4 sp. Rep from * across, ch 3, sk ch-4 sp, tr in last sc. Turn.

Row 4: Ch 3, dc in tr, ch 3, sk next sc, sc in each of next 3 sc, *ch 3, (dc, ch 2, dc) in ch-7 sp, ch 3, sk next sc, sc in each of next 3 sc. Rep from * across, ch 3, work 2 dc in 4th ch of t-ch. Turn.

Row 5: Ch 3, 2 dc in 1st dc, ch 4, sk next sc, sc in next sc, *ch 4, sk ch-3 sp, 5 dc in next ch-1 sp, ch 4, sk next sc, sc in next sc. Rep from *across, ch 4, work 3 dc in top of t-ch. Turn.

Row 6: Ch 1, sc in each of 1st 3 dc, *ch 7, sk next ch-4 sp, sc in each of next 5 dc. Rep from * across, ch 7, sc in last each of last 3 dc. Turn.

Row 7: Ch 1, sc in each of 1st 2 dc, *ch 3, (dc, ch 2, dc) in ch-7 sp, ch 3, sk next sc, sc in each of next 3 sc. Rep from * across, ending with sc in last 2 sc. Turn.

Rep Rows 2–7 14 more times. Cut yarn, leaving an 8-in. tail, pull through last loop and tighten. Do not weave the tail in.

SECOND HALF OF THE SHAWL BODY

Beginning on opposite side of foundation ch, work Rows 1–7. Rep Rows 2–7 14 more times. Cut yarn, leaving an 8-in. tail, pull through last loop and tighten. Do not weave the tail in.

TOP BORDER

Beginning at upper left edge, attach yarn to shawl with a sl st.

Row 1: Ch 1, sc in each of 1st 2 sc, 3 sc in ch-3 sp, 8 dc in ch-1 sp, *2 dc in next ch-3 sp, sc in each of next 3 sc, 2 sc in next ch-3 sp, 8 sc in ch-1 sp. Rep from * across, 3 dc in last ch-3 sp, sc in each of last 2 sc. Turn.

Row 2: Ch 1, sc in 1st sc, ch 6, sk 3 dc, 2 dc in next dc, ch 2, 2 dc in next dc, *ch 6, sk 3 sc, sc in next sc, ch 6, sk 3 dc, 2 dc in next dc, ch 2, 2 dc in next dc. Rep from * to end, ch 6, sc in last sc. Turn.

Row 3: Ch 1, sc in 1st sc, *ch 7, (2 dc, ch 2, 2 dc) in ch-2 sp, ch 7, sc in next sc. Rep from * across. Turn.

Row 4: Ch 1, sc in 1st sc, *ch 8, (2 dc, ch 2, 2 dc) in ch-2 sp, ch 8, sc in next sc. Rep from * across, end with ch 8. Turn.

Row 5: Ch 1, sc in 1st sc, *ch 9, 2 dc in ch-2 sp, ch 3, sl st in 2nd ch from hook (picot made), ch 1, 2 dc in same ch-2 sp, ch 9, sc in next sc. Rep from * across.

Cut yarn, leaving an 8-in. tail, pull through the last loop and tighten. Do not weave the tail in.

BOTTOM BORDER

Rep as for Top Border, along bottom edge.

Weave in all loose ends. Block if desired.

The Traveling Shawl

I am so lucky. I think I'd be friends with my daughter-in-law, Genevieve, even if she wasn't married to my son and the mother of my (amazing, genius, fantastic) grandchildren. When they announced that Gen had gotten a great job halfway across the country, I was happy for her and excited about this new adventure for her and the family. But I was also sad for myself because I knew that I would miss them all terribly.

When the opportunity came to design a shawl for this book, I knew immediately whom I would crochet for: Genevieve. This shawl is light and airy, for cool nights in warm climes. It's beautiful without being fussy, just like Gen. And it's worked with love in every stitch. The hope is that this new journey will be a wonderful adventure.

—KATHLEEN TAYLOR
Reddington, South Dakota

BLESSING FOR GEN

Worked with love in every stitch,
light and airy into which
you'll enfold yourself when I'm not there,
Always knowing that I care.

—KATHLEEN TAYLOR
REDDINGTON, SOUTH DAKOTA

T HE COLOR AND SYMBOLISM OF STITCHES IN a prayer shawl help to convey sentiments to whomever receives it. Use colors, numbers, gemstones, and fragrances to give symbolic meaning to your shawls. Here I've used a topaz-colored yarn, which suggests warmth, sunlight, and energy.

FROM
Vicky Galo
Berlin, Connecticut

TOPAZ SHAWL

Skill Level
Easy

Finished Measurements
18 in. x 65 in., excluding fringe

Yarn
- Medium Weight Yarn (CYCA 4), approx. 1,240 yd. Orange
- Shawl shown in Red Heart® Symphony (100% acrylic; 310 yd./3.5 oz), 4 skeins #4906 Persimmon

Hook
- Size L/11/8.00 mm (or size needed to obtain gauge)

Gauge
- 3 loops and 5 rows = 4 in. in patt st. Gauge is not critical in this pattern.

Note: Use two strands held together throughout.

DIRECTIONS
Ch 65 (multiple of 5).

Row 1: Sc in 5th ch from hook, *ch 4, sk 4 ch, sc in next ch. Rep from * to end. Ch 5, turn. (13 loops)

Row 2: Sc in 1st loop, *ch 4, sc in next loop. Rep from * to end. Ch 5, turn.

Rep Row 2 for pattern until shawl is 65 in., stretched, or desired length. Do not ch 5 at end of last row. End off.

FRINGE
Cut 104 12-in. lengths of yarn. Fold each strand in half, attach four strands of fringe in each loop of short end. Tie groups of 4 in an overhand knot close to the shawl.

I saw the picture of the Cape Cod Shawl in *The Prayer Shawl Companion* and I had to make a crocheted version for my cousin, who is caring for her dying husband. It was my hope that sharing something of the strength and happiness I get from being on the Cape would help her in her journey.

FROM
Joanne Tyndall
Shrewsbury, Massachusetts

CAPE COD SHAWL

Skill Level
Easy

Finished Measurements
24 in. x 30 in.

Yarn
- Bulky Weight Yarn (CYCA 5), approx. 762 yd. Blue
- Shawl shown in Classic Elite Yarns Montera (50% llama/50% wool; 127 yd./3.5 oz.), 6 skeins #3829 Aqua Ice

Hook
- Size K/10.5/6.5 mm (or size needed to obtain gauge)

Gauge
- 12 dc and 7 rows = 4 in. in patt st

Special Stitches
- **Fpdc** = front post double crochet
- **Bpdc** = back post double crochet

Note: Ch-3 counts as 1 dc throughout.

DIRECTIONS
Ch 70 (odd multiple of 4 + 2 for foundation ch).

Row 1: Dc in 4th ch from hook and in each ch across. Ch 3, turn. (68 dc)

Row 2: Sk 1st dc, fpdc in each of next 3 dc, bpdc in each of next 4 dc, *fpdc in each of next 4 dc, bpdc in each of next 4 dc. Rep from * to last 4 dc, fpdc in each of next 3 dc, dc in last dc. Ch 3, turn.

Row 3: Sk 1st dc, bpdc around each of next 3 fpdc, fpdc around each of next 4 bpdc, *bpdc around each of next 4 fpdc, fpdc around each of next 4 bpdc. Rep from * to last 4 dc, bpdc in each of next 3 fpdc, dc in last dc. Ch 3, turn.

Rep Rows 2 and 3 for pattern until work measures 30 in. or desired length. End off. Weave in ends.

CROCHETING ABBREVIATIONS

Beg—beginning

CC—contrasting color

Ch—chain

Dc—double crochet

Dc2tog—double crochet 2 together, a decrease

Dec—decrease

FPdc—front post double crochet

FPtr—front post treble crochet

G—gram

Hdc—half double crochet

Inc—increase

MC—main color

Mm—millimeter(s)

Oz—ounce

Rep—repeat

Rev sc or crab st—reverse single crochet

Rnd—round

RS—right side

Sc—single crochet

Sc2tog—single crochet 2 together, a decrease

Sk—skip

Sl st—slip stitch

T-ch—turning chain

Tog—together

Tr—treble crochet

WS—wrong side

Yo—yarn over

* The master list from the Craft Yarn Council of America is available at www.craftyarncouncil.com/crochet.html

STANDARD YARN WEIGHTS

YARN WEIGHT SYMBOL	YARN WEIGHT NAMES	TYPE OF YARNS IN CATEGORY	CROCHET GAUGE* (RANGES IN SINGLE CROCHET TO 4 INCH)	RECOMMENDED HOOK (IN METRIC SIZE RANGE)	RECOMMENDED HOOK (IN U.S. SIZE RANGE)
0	Lace	Fingering 10-count crochet thread	32–42 double crochets**	Steel*** 1.6–1.4 mm	Steel*** 6, 7, 8 Regular hook B–1
1	Super Fine	Sock, Fingering, Baby	21–32 sts	2.25–3.5 mm	B–1 to E–4
2	Fine	Sport, Baby	16–20 sts	3.5–4.5 mm	E–4 to 7
3	Light	DK, Light Worsted	12–17 sts	4.5–5.5 mm	7 to I–9
4	Medium	Worsted, Afghan, Aran	11–14 sts	5.5–6.5 mm	I–9 to K–10½
5	Bulky	Chunky, Craft, Rug	8–11 sts	6.5–9 mm	K–10½ to M–13
6	Super Bulky	Bulky, Roving	5–9 sts	9 mm and larger	M–13 and larger

*   GUIDELINES ONLY: The above reflect the most commonly used gauges and needle or hook sizes for specific yarn categories.

** Lace weight yarns are usually knitted or crocheted on larger needles and hooks to create lacy, openwork patterns. Accordingly, a gauge range is difficult to determine. Always follow the gauge stated in your pattern.

*** Steel crochet hooks are sized differently from regular hooks—the higher the number, the smaller the hook, which is the reverse of regular hook sizing

Look for these other THREADS Selects booklets at www.taunton.com and wherever crafts are sold.

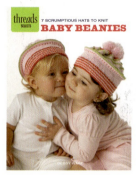

Baby Beanies
Debby Ware

EAN: 9781621137634
8 ½ x 10 ⅞, 32 pages
Product# 078001
$9.95 U.S., $11.95 Can.

Fair Isle Flower Garden
Kathleen Taylor

EAN: 9781621137702
8 ½ x 10 ⅞, 32 pages
Product# 078008
$9.95 U.S., $11.95 Can.

Fair Isle Hats, Scarves, Mittens & Gloves
Kathleen Taylor

EAN: 9781621137719
8 ½ x 10 ⅞, 32 pages
Product# 078009
$9.95 U.S., $11.95 Can.

Lace Socks
Kathleen Taylor

EAN: 9781621137894
8 ½ x 10 ⅞, 32 pages
Product# 078012
$9.95 U.S., $11.95 Can.

Colorwork Socks
Kathleen Taylor

EAN: 9781621137740
8 ½ x 10 ⅞, 32 pages
Product# 078011
$9.95 U.S., $11.95 Can.

DIY Bride Cakes & Sweets
Khris Cochran

EAN: 9781621137665
8 ½ x 10 ⅞, 32 pages
Product# 078004
$9.95 U.S., $11.95 Can.

DIY Bride Beautiful Bouquets
Khris Cochran

EAN: 9781621137672
8 ½ x 10 ⅞, 32 pages
Product# 078005
$9.95 U.S., $11.95 Can.

Bead Necklaces
Susan Beal

EAN: 9781621137641
8 ½ x 10 ⅞, 32 pages
Product# 078002
$9.95 U.S., $11.95 Can.

Drop Earrings
Susan Beal

EAN: 9781621137658
8 ½ x 10 ⅞, 32 pages
Product# 078003
$9.95 U.S., $11.95 Can.

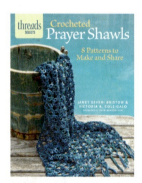

Crochet Prayer Shawls
Janet Severi Bristow & Victoria A. Cole-Galo

EAN: 9781621137689
8 ½ x 10 ⅞, 32 pages
Product# 078006
$9.95 U.S., $11.95 Can.

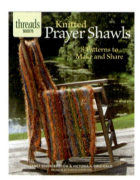

Knitted Prayer Shawls
Janet Severi Bristow & Victoria A. Cole-Galo

EAN: 9781621137696
8 ½ x 10 ⅞, 32 pages
Product# 078007
$9.95 U.S., $11.95 Can.

Shawlettes
Jean Moss

EAN: 9781621137726
8 ½ x 10 ⅞, 32 pages
Product# 078010
$9.95 U.S., $11.95 Can.